Carol Adams

How they lived in

a Medieval Castle

Illustrated by Gareth Adamson

Lutterworth Press · Guildford · Surrey · England

About a thousand years ago, in what we call 'the Middle Ages', the rulers of northern France built the first castles, to control their people and defend their lands. These 'Normans', as we call them, invaded England in 1066, and built castles there too. For the next four hundred years or so, many castles were built in the countries of western Europe.

Castles belonged either to the king or to his barons. The king usually owned many castles on his royal estates. He granted other estates to his barons. A wealthy baron might own vast estates with several castles, each guarded by a band of soldiers who could put down any rebellion and beat off any attack by the baron's enemies. In return for the grants of land, the barons had to fight for the king and provide him with soldiers. We now call this arrangement 'feudalism'. The king and the barons were always on the move, visiting each castle in turn to keep control of their affairs.

Castles were built on carefully chosen sites: to overlook a town or a port, to control a river or a frontier. The first castles were made of wood, but soon stone was used for greater strength and more endurance. As new, more powerful weapons were made, so new and better ways of building castles had to be found, making them stronger and safer.

As well as being strongholds, castles were also the homes of the barons, their families and their servants. A household might number a hundred people, so living space was important too. The early castles were uncomfortable, grim places, but as life became more settled and peaceful, more attention could be paid to comfort. Lords made their castles pleasanter with more rooms, more furniture, and up-to-date improvements.

A castle built in the fourteenth century, to the latest standards of defence and comfort, was very different from one built three hundred years earlier. Many castles, however, were old ones which were altered and added to over the centuries. It is common to find that a castle was built in three or four stages.

This book is about an imaginary castle, some seven hundred years ago. The castle belongs to an English baron. Imagine going back to meet the people who lived their everyday lives there.

Lidworth Castle belongs to Sir Guy, a rich and powerful
baron who owns all the land for miles around, and another
castle in the north. Lidworth's great stone tower, thick walls
and moat were built by Sir Guy's ancestors, but the new
round defence towers, the fine new Hall and chapel and the
laid-out gardens have only been finished this year. The
castle is now up-to-date and newly whitewashed.

Joan is Sir Guy's niece. While Sir Guy is often away from home serving the King, Joan stays at Lidworth with his wife, Lady Anne. Now twelve years old, Joan has been at Lidworth since she was eight, learning the duties and responsibilities of a lady. For one day, like Lady Anne, she will have to take charge of a castle household while her husband is away.

Thomas is a scullion. He works in the scullery next to the
kitchen, cleaning and fetching and carrying all the dishes
and cooking pots. He has always lived at Lidworth as his
parents are both servants here. The work is very hard and
Thomas, who is only nine, often gets beaten by the cook for
playing about with the other children or for stealing food.

Over a hundred people live at Lidworth, each with their special job to do. After Sir Guy and Lady Anne, the most important person is the steward, Sir Roger. He manages everyday affairs and sees that everyone does their job properly. He is a rich knight himself, and when Sir Guy is away he runs his business affairs for him.

Next in importance is the chamberlain, who is in charge of supplying the food for everyone. Under him work the cook, the pantler (who is in charge of the bread), the butler (who looks after the drink), the chandler (who keeps the store of candles), the maids, the scullions and the rest of the kitchen staff.

The chaplain is the castle's priest. As well as holding services in the chapel, he writes Sir Guy's letters for him and teaches the pages their lessons. The 'keeper of the wardrobe' is in charge of the stores and keeps the accounts which are written out on scrolls of rolled-up paper called the 'Household Roll'.

There are seamstresses, laundresses, lady's maids and children's nurses all working in the household.

Those who spend their time working outside in the bailey are important too. The armourers repair and clean the armour and weapons in their workshop; the blacksmiths make shoes for the horses, who are looked after by the grooms; the bowyers and fletchers make bows and arrows, while the masons, thatchers and craftsmen work on the buildings. There are other servants to tend the animals in their pens, the bees and the gardens.

Soldiers live in the castle too. There are knights who serve
Sir Guy and go to fight beside him. Their horses and armour
have to be looked after – and their squires' equipment, too.

Then there are the soldiers who guard the castle itself:
archers and crossbowmen, and the sentries who keep watch
day and night along the walls and on the towers. It is many
years since any enemy barons attacked Lidworth but now
there is trouble in the north; the guards must always be
ready. The soldiers spend a lot of their time practising with
their weapons in the bailey so that they will be fit and skilful
when they have to fight.

The Great Hall is the centre of life at Lidworth: the place where everyone meets. It is new and spacious, and everyone likes it better than the old Hall in the Great Tower, so dark and cramped. The upper part of the walls is plastered, and the lower part is wainscotted (covered with wooden panelling), for warmth. The wainscot is brightly painted in red and yellow. There is a large fireplace and a chimney to get rid of the smoke, though the room is often still smoky because of all the draughts. The windows have no glass in them – glass is very expensive – so at night or in bad weather the wooden shutters are closed, making it dark. Around the Hall are wooden chests and aumbries, or cupboards, for storing dishes. There are benches to sit on. The only comfortable chairs are set at one end, for the lord and lady.

The banqueting hall at Castle Hedingham in Essex

The castle day starts early – at around five, or earlier if it is
light. Most of the servants and soldiers have been sleeping
in the Hall, either on benches or on the floor. They sleep in
their clothes and wrap their cloaks around them. The floor
is covered with rushes and nobody thinks it is
uncomfortable – none of them has ever slept in a bed (only
Sir Guy's family have beds). They are used to the dirt, the
dogs and cats and mice that run about, and the bones and
scraps of food dropped on the floor. The Hall is noisy when
dozens of men lie snoring after a hard day's work and plenty
of ale.

Joan is woken by one of the servant girls in the dormitory
where she sleeps with the maids and her cousins. She sleeps
on a straw mattress on a wooden bed which is covered over
to make a seat during the day. She washes her hands and
face at a stone basin in the corner. The maid has brought
water from the well, and Joan uses soap made from mutton
fat and wood ash, scented with herbs. Once a week she has
a bath in a large wooden tub, and as water is precious, it is
shared by all the females.

Built into the wall at the end of the room is a garderobe, or
lavatory. There is a round wooden seat over a long chute
which leads down into a ditch outside. This is cleaned by
one of the servants.

A maid helps Joan to dress. She puts on woollen stockings,
a linen shift, and over this her long woollen dress, or tunic,
and an overtunic on top. She fastens her tunic with a silver
brooch, a present from Lady Anne. She wears her hair
loose, but when she is older it will be plaited.

Sir Guy and Lady Anne sleep in the solar, their private room, built at one end of the Hall. It is the most comfortable room in the castle. There is a large four-poster bed with curtains round it to keep out the draughts. They sleep on a feather mattress with linen sheets and fur covers. Because their bed is warm they take off their clothes to sleep and Sir Guy wears a nightcap.

The room has a fireplace, a carpet, and brightly coloured tapestries on the walls. Sir Guy bought these from merchants who bring back beautiful materials from the Middle East. Lady Anne buys silk and damask from them for her clothes. Above the bed is the family coat of arms. During the day, the solar is the lord's living-room, and there are several wooden chests where clothes and documents are put away. There is a wooden chair by the fire, and plates and dishes of silver. The window has glass in it, so the room is much lighter than the Hall, and there is a large window seat.

When a servant has got everything ready, Sir Guy washes in his basin with water poured from a jug called an 'ewer', and is shaved by his page. The page has to take great care – for the shaving knife is not very sharp, and if his hand slips Sir Guy will be in a furious rage.

The page helps Sir Guy to dress. He puts on linen breeches
and woollen stockings, called 'hose', a long loose-fitting
woollen tunic, and over this his 'surcoat' which is lined with
ermine. On his head he wears a linen cap. His clothes are
warm and comfortable but brightly coloured in green and
gold, with fashionably flared sleeves.

Lady Anne's clothes are similar to her husband's. Over her
stockings and petticoat she wears a long tunic fastened at
the waist with a girdle, and on top goes a fur-trimmed
mantle. For feasts or special occasions she may wear a gown
of silk or velvet. Her maid plaits her hair and covers it with
a wimple of stiff linen. Both she and her husband wear soft
leather shoes with pointed toes.

Thomas sleeps on the kitchen floor close to the fire, curled up next to one of the dogs. He sleeps in his clothes so he doesn't have to get dressed in the morning. He is one of the first to wake in the castle. He dips his hands and face in the big tub of water, and that is all the washing he does, except in summer when it gets very hot in the kitchen and the scullions jump into tubs of water out in the yard to cool off.

Thomas has to fetch water from the well, light the fire and heat washing water before Sir Guy and his family get up. Then there is the fetching and carrying for breakfast, taking bread and ale into the Hall. Pieces of white wheaten bread must be put on the lord's table, and there is coarse brown rye bread for everyone else.

The day starts with a service in the chapel for Sir Guy's family, and the most important household officials also attend. Joan likes listening to the priest chanting the Mass in the quiet of the dark cool chapel, and looking up at the fine stone arches and large windows. After Mass, breakfast is eaten quickly, and is the smallest meal of the day. Joan has milk with her bread and Sir Guy has a cup of wine, but most people have a mug of ale. Then everyone goes off to start the day's work.

Sir Guy is in the Hall with Sir Roger settling legal matters
with some of the tenants who live on his manors. One man
is behind with the work he must do on Sir Guy's land. There
is a quarrel to settle between two brothers over which one
should inherit their father's land. Another tenant seeks
permission for his daughter to marry. One man is being
fined for poaching. Legal agreements, written on rolls of
parchment, are brought from the treasury (the room where
money and valuables are kept), to check up on the tenants'
rights, and the chaplain keeps a record of the morning's
business.

Lady Anne is busy in the maids' chamber in charge of her sewing women. One woman is working on a fine silk robe for Lady Anne. Another is finishing some wraps for the baby, who is being rocked in her wooden cradle by the nurse. Some of the women are spinning thread to be woven into cloth, and others are making woollen tunics. Several damsels are embroidering a new hanging for the wall, and Lady Anne, well-known for her skill at this art, closely checks their work.

Next Lady Anne takes her maid to the garden where she grows herbs and flowers. More lavender must be picked and placed in bowls in the solar to keep the air sweet. She orders the maid to pick herbs – parsley, sage, garlic, mustard and fennel – for ointments and medicines. The herbs will be ground up with a pestle and mortar and then mixed with honey and vinegar. Lady Anne will use them to treat cuts and bruises and to soothe aches and pains. When anyone is sick, she decides what is to be done.

A messenger arrives with news of Lady Anne's son, who is living in her cousin's household as a squire. He was sent away from Lidworth six years ago, aged eight, to be a page; now he is learning the duties of a knight. Lady Anne has several boys in her household who are training as pages and squires, and she must make sure they attend to their lessons. She gives the messenger some letters to deliver when he has rested. She sends a gift to her son, and some money to the local nunnery.

Joan spends the morning at her lessons. She is learning to write with a quill pen. The chaplain helps her. When he is satisfied with her work, she goes to practise her harp-playing and her singing with the pages. Nearby two squires are being taught Latin. Their lessons are a little harder than hers as they are older. When she was ten, Joan was betrothed to one of the squires, called Richard, and after her fourteenth birthday, they will be married. The match was arranged by Joan's parents, as are all marriages for the daughters of knights and lords and wealthy men. Joan does not want to be married yet, but she knows that when the time comes she must do as her parents say.

The kitchen is hot, noisy and full of activity. During Lent,
and on special days each year, there are Church rules to say
that no one may eat meat – only fish, eggs and vegetables
are allowed. Today is a 'meat' day, though, and a joint of
venison is being roasted over the fire, while one of the boys
turns the spit. Some of the kitchen maids are pounding pork
to make rissoles. Others are grinding spices – ginger,
pepper, cinnamon, cloves and mace. The meat is stored in
salt in the castle basement and often starts to go bad before
it is eaten. The spices are used to disguise the rotten taste.

The baker's lads are putting loaves into the oven, and the ale wife is brewing ale from barley. The cook is supervising the making of a lark's tongue pie, a great delicacy of meat wrapped in a pastry case, called a 'coffin'. Eel stew is cooking in the cauldron. Thomas is helping to make blancmange – a savoury dish made from beef fat.

Dinner time is ten o'clock, and this is the main meal of the day. Everyone is hungry from their morning's work. Sir Guy and his family sit at a table at the end of the Hall, raised on a platform, or 'dais'. This is the 'high table', and it is covered with a white cloth and laid with silver spoons, salt, and dishes and cups of silver and pewter. The rest of the household sit at trestle tables which can be taken apart and lifted away after the meal. Their cups are earthenware, their spoons are made of horn, and there is no cloth. Everyone has a 'trencher' – a thick slice of stale bread, used as a plate. People cut their meat with their knives, which they carry in their belts between meals, and they eat with their fingers. There are no forks.

First Sir Guy and Lady Anne wash their hands in bowls of water brought to them by a servant. Other people use a basin and ewer on a stand at the end of the Hall.

This picture was drawn in the fifteenth century to illustrate the biblical story of Job. He is shown dressed as a fifteenth-century lord feasting with his sons at 'high table'. Note the table cloth, the simple plates and beakers, the pieces of bread and the knives.

My head at meals I must not scratch as though I sought a flea.
My eyes they shall not blink nor should they watery be.
I must not blow my nose too loud lest my master hear
I must not spit too far nor scratch my ear.
With my mouth I must not squirt nor spout.
Nor lick with tongue a dish, the last bit to get out.
My teeth nor nails I must not pick with knife
To put it in were peril of my life.
When done with fish and meat and broth
Clean knife with bread and not upon the cloth
Beware lest hand on board cloth goes;
On which I must not wipe my hands or nose.

from: Rules for a Young Gentleman at Table

The pages serve the lord and his guests on bended knee.
They must know how to carve and serve the food correctly,
and they must remember their manners. The roasted meat
and the pies are only for the high table, and here the butler
serves wine. Each dish of food is shared between two
people. On the lower tables the food is not so fine – stew
and rissoles – and there is ale to drink. If Sir Guy is in a
good mood, he may send some tasty scraps to his servants.
The food looks very colourful because it has been dyed: the
meat is yellow with saffron, the soup is red with blood, and
the pies are green with parsley.

Soon the Hall is noisy and cheerful. Hungry dogs jump
about the tables. The left-overs may be thrown to them, or
may be gathered by Lady Anne's almoner to give to the
poor at the castle gates. The scullions are still hard at work
in the kitchen but they manage to snatch some meat on its
way to the Hall.

After dinner Sir Guy is going hunting with his guests – an
official from the King's Court, and an abbot who has called
at Lidworth on his way to visit some of his abbey's lands.
Lady Anne is going on the hunt too – she is very fond of
hunting. The grooms have the horses ready and off they all
go across the drawbridge. Sir Guy's huntsman and the
hounds lead the way towards the forest. Perhaps they will
bring back a deer for tomorrow's dinner. Sir Guy goes
hunting most days when he is at home.

The people of the castle get back to work. The armourers
are cleaning mail shirts by rolling them in barrels of sand.
They rub the helmets with pumice stone to make them
clean and shining. Then the swords must be sharpened on a
grinder. Joan comes down to watch the carpenter who is
building a new dovecote for Lady Anne. Thomas has been
sent to collect the eggs from the chicken pens, but he stops
to talk to the thatcher's lad who is helping to mend the roof
of the barn.

In the exercise yard a group of squires enjoy a favourite sport: they are learning how to joust, under the guidance of an older knight. Although the squires still have to wait on Sir Guy, just as the pages do, the most important part of their training now is to learn the art of war. They must know how to wear armour: how to ride and fight in it: how to use a knight's weapons – the sword and the lance. Then, too, they must know how to shoot with the longbow and the crossbow and how to use the weapons of a man at arms – for one day they may have to lead an army into battle and will need to understand each soldier's job as well as being skilful fighters themselves.

Today they are practising for the day when, as knights, they will show off their skill and strength at tournaments. It is very difficult to hold the heavy lance and at the same time to guide the horse into the correct position for striking at the opponent. They practise by charging at a target called a 'quintain'. One squire falls off, but he is quite used to this and is not hurt. Another hits the target exactly right, ducking at the proper moment, and there are loud cheers.

The squires are looking forward to the next tournament which Sir Guy will hold at Lidworth. Knights come from all round this part of the country to show off their skills at combat, and it is a very colourful sight to see them all in their coats of arms. Joan enjoys the tournaments, especially the music and feasting afterwards, but Thomas always feels a little envious that he will never be able to wear an armour or own a horse.

The castle soldiers are busy down at the gatehouse making sure that all their defences are in good working order. During the day the drawbridge is left down for people, horses, carts and so on to cross the moat and go in and out of the castle. At night it is pulled up by two great chains. The heavy door is locked securely with great iron bolts, and two portcullises are wound down into position, one on the inside of the door, and the other on the outside. Above the entrance are six murder holes so that the defenders can pour boiling oil or drop stones onto the heads of attacking enemies, and can tip down water to quench any fire the attackers might start.

Some soldiers live in the gatehouse and take it in turns to guard the entrance day and night. Others keep guard in the round defence towers built into the walls, or patrol the wall walk with its protective battlements and arrow slits. A few of the soldiers stay in the great tower and keep a look-out; from the top they can see for miles around. Lidworth was first built in the days when barons were often at war with one another, and so everyone lived in the great tower. Now the household would only go there for safety if the castle were attacked.

At about five o'clock the sound of the horn announces the return of the hunting party. They all make their way to the Hall for supper, a smaller meal than dinner, with dishes made from eggs and cheese, and pies filled with fruit from the garden. Only on special occasions, or if someone very important is visiting, will there be a feast with lots of food.

The Hall is lit by candles made from rushes which have been twisted and dipped in fat. More ale and wine are drunk, and as everyone relaxes in the noisy smoky room it is time for the evening's recreation. A group of musicians is staying at Lidworth for a few days and they play their flutes, guitars, trumpets and drums. Some of the household dance to the music. Thomas and some of the other boys are having a wrestling match in one corner, while the pages are having just as rough a game of 'Hoodman Blind'. At the high table Sir Guy's jester is making him laugh while Lady Anne is enjoying the singing of her minstrel. The steward is discussing business with the Court official, and the chamberlain is listening to the latest news from the messenger.

Joan goes up to the solar with the lady's maid to play draughts. Some of the other children are playing skittles, and two pages are having a game of chess, while another group secretly plays dice.

The evening is short because once it is dark, to rest is better than burning candles. Soon everyone except the soldiers on guard is asleep after a hard day's work.

Life at Lidworth was much the same as life in hundreds of
other castles at this time – some larger and grander, some
smaller and more old-fashioned. Occasionally the peace
was interrupted by war, or by a disaster such as plague or
famine; but more and more, as time went on, castles
became places where people lived a peaceful community
life, rather than military strongholds. Barons like Sir Guy
no longer kept their own armies and fought each other;
instead they were united under the king, whom they all
obeyed. Gunpowder was discovered, and with it came new
weapons which were so powerful that castle walls and moats
no longer meant safety. The lords moved into fashionable
new houses instead, and eventually castles were not built
any more.

INDEX

PHOTOGRAPHS   The photograph on page 8 is used by courtesy of the National Monuments Record, London. The photograph on page 22 is used by permission of the British Library (Harley ms, 2838, f.45).

First published 1981   ISBN 0 7188–2439–3   All Rights Reserved

Photoset in Great Britain by
Nene Phototypesetters Ltd, Northampton

Printed in Hong Kong by
Colorcraft Ltd.